Top Notes

T0363053

Raymond Gaita's

Romulus, My Father

Study notes for Standard English:
Module C 2015-2020 HSC

Bruce Pattinson

——A——
FIVE SENSES
PUBLICATION

Five Senses Education Pty Ltd
2/195 Prospect Highway
Seven Hills 2147
New South Wales
Australia

Pattinson, Bruce,
Top Notes – Romulus, My Father
ISBN 978 -1- 74130 – 999 – 7

CONTENTS

INTRODUCTION TO THE TOP NOTES SERIES

Top Notes are designed with the high school student in mind. They are written in an easy to read manner yet discuss the important ideas and issues that you need to understand so you can successfully undertake your English HSC examinations.

They are written by practising teachers who have years of experience. Each Top Notes contains many helpful tips for the course and examination. Top Notes focus specifically on the student's needs and they examine each text in the context of the module and elective to which it has been allocated.

Each text includes:

- Notes on the specific module
- Plot summary
- Character analysis
- Setting
- Thematic concerns
- Language studies
- Essay questions and a plan
- Other textual material
- Additional questions
- Useful quotes

I am sure you will find these Top Notes useful in your studies of English.

Bruce Pattinson
Series Editor

THE STANDARD COURSE

This is a brief analysis of the Standard course to ensure you are completely familiar with what you are attempting in the examination. If in any doubt at all, check with your teacher or the Board of Studies website.

The Standard Course requires you to have studied:

- Four prescribed texts. This means four texts from the list given to your teacher by the Board of Studies.

- For each of the texts, one must come from each of the following four categories.
  - drama
  - poetry
  - prose fiction (novel usually)
  - nonfiction or media or film or multimedia texts. (Multimedia are CD ROMs, websites, etc.)

- A range of related texts of your own choosing. These are part of your Area of Study, Module A and Module C. Do not confuse these with the main set text you are studying. This is very important.

Area of Study: Discovery

Module A	*Module B*	*Module C*
Experience through Language	**Close Study of Text**	**Texts and Society**
Electives	*Electives*	*Electives*
▪ Distinctive Voices OR ▪ Distinctively Visual	▪ Drama OR ▪ Prose Fiction OR ▪ Nonfiction, Film, Media, Multimedia OR ▪ Poetry	▪ Exploring Interactions OR ▪ Exploring Transitions

You must study the Area of Study and EACH of Modules A, B and C

There are options within EACH of these that your school will select.

TEXTS AND SOCIETY

ELECTIVE ONE: Exploring Interactions

The "Texts and Society" module, Module C, requires you to examine and analyse texts which arise from or represent a particular situation or context. The syllabus states that, "Modules...emphasise particular aspects of shaping meaning and representation, questions of textual integrity, and ways in which texts are valued."[1] Texts and Society is a module that asks students to:

- Explore and analyse texts in a specific situation

- Examine the ways texts communicate information, ideas, bodies of knowledge, attitudes and belief systems in ways particular to specific areas of society.

HSC PRESCRIPTIONS 2015-20 P14

The first elective in Texts and Society is Exploring Interactions and this is the particular focus when studying *Romulus, My Father* by Raymond Gaita (1998). The Module's focus must be kept in mind as well as the elective.

The idea of interactions should be explored in and through the text. That is, with reference to content and techniques. It can be explored thematically and can also relate to the characters, their interactions and the dynamics of relationships.

---

1 http://www.boardofstudies.nsw.edu.au/syllabus_hsc/pdf_doc/english-prescriptions-2015-20.pdf

Interactions should also be explored through the textual form, in this case, Gaita's choice of filial memoir, a non-fiction genre. In this way, the Module's mention of "Text" assumes significance. This focus on textual form and techniques holds true for your approach to, not only your prescribed text, but also your related text choices. Ask how the poetic, filmic, narrative, dramatic or other specific techniques linked to the textual form of your related material, contribute to representing interactions within the given text.

The rubric for this elective prescribes that,

"students explore and analyse a variety of texts that portray the ways in which individuals live, interact and communicate in a range of social contexts. These contexts may include the home, cultural, friendship and sporting groups, the workplace and the digital world. Through exploring their prescribed text and texts of their own choosing, students consider how acts of communication can shape, challenge or transform attitudes and beliefs, identities and behaviours. In their responding and composing, students develop their understanding of how the social context of individuals' interactions can affect perceptions of ourselves and others, relationships and society." HTTP://WWW.BOARDOFSTUDIES. NSW.EDU.AU/SYLLABUS_HSC/PDF_DOC/ENGLISH-PRESCRIPTIONS-2015-20.PDF

After studying this text, you will have,

- Analysed a variety of texts
- Explored how these texts portray the ways individuals live, interact and communicate in a range of social contexts.
- Understood that contexts may be personal, social, historical and cultural. They can include home,

friendship and sporting groups, the workplace and the digital world.

- Considered how acts of communication can shape, challenge and transform attitudes, beliefs, identities and behaviours.
- Developed an understanding of how the social context of interactions can affect perceptions of ourselves and others, relationships and society.

This module does require you to find other texts. The exam question for this module will usually ask you to write an essay, which would involve forming an answer to a specific essay question, and using your interpretation of the text to draw conclusions about the essay subject.

The exam question will focus on the ideas in the rubric which were summarized on the previous page. Always remember that the focus must be on Exploring Interactions, textual forms and features and links to society.

Despite the questions you receive in your exams and assessments, your marks will improve if you can:

- Analyse and interpret the text instead of retelling
- Discuss the intentions of the composer(s) and the various effects on the responder
- Identify techniques and integrate an analysis of the effect of techniques into your response
- Keep a focus on the Module, Elective and discuss the interactions in the textual material and links between text and related material.

STUDYING A NON-FICTION TEXT

The medium of a text is very important. If a text is non-fiction this means that its purpose is to report events, situations or trends. The composer does not create, but rather chooses the events of the story and the events have actually happened. The composer shapes the text by choosing which events to include and how he or she portrays them. The manner of this portrayal will depend on the composer's purpose. The composer adds his or her perspective to the description of the events. This bias will have an effect on the way the responder perceives the story. The responder can choose to accept or reject the composer's **version** of events.

Realism is created in a non-fiction text by the inclusion of actual people, events or situations. These may be reported objectively or subjectively.

The creator of a non-fiction text, in a similar manner to writers of fiction, may create interest through the use of **narrative techniques**. These are the elements of the text which are manipulated by the composer to present their ideas effectively. When you are discussing how the composer represents his ideas, you MUST discuss techniques. Language techniques are sometimes referred to as **stylistic devices**.

Many of the techniques used in non-fiction are identical to those used in fiction.

NARRATIVE TECHNIQUES

Structure: how is the text organised?

Punctuation: what features are used and why? Look for patterns in character speech

Characterisation

Narrative Voice: and what is its effect?

Dialogue: how do characters speak and what does this show. How is silence used? Who speaks most?

Symbols and motifs: how is repetition of image/idea used to maximise the effect?

Narrative Techniques

Humour: puns, one liners, black humour, irony, sarcasm...

Sentences: length and type

Imagery, allusions

Use of questioning: rhetoric

Tone: of narration and characters

Setting-Real and symbolic

Themes e.g. Conflict: the action, Man vs man, Man vs nature, and/ or Man vs himself

Vocabulary choice eg Emotive language

Aural techniques: repetition, onomatopoeia, alliteration, assonance

BIOGRAPHY & AUTOBIOGRAPHY

Biography is a written account of a person's life or the study of the lives of individuals (Macquarie Dictionary) and Gaita's *Romulus, My Father* is usually referred to as a biography in the critical literature. Indeed, the story is told in a biographical manner with one individual narrating the life story of another. *Romulus, My Father,* however, is more than this. It is also a text that focuses on social trends, philosophical ideas and shows aspects of Australia. Many of the elements of biography are detailed in the next section and the notes are relevant to both biography and autobiography

This text is also partly **autobiography** which is defined in the Oxford Dictionary as 'one's life written by oneself'. An autobiography is a personal recount of a life or events in a life and it generally has a reflective tone. Because it is personal the text usually reflects the 'self' of the individual.

Autobiography is a popular form of writing as it gives the individual full control over what aspects of their life they share with the audience. This can lead to omissions or situations where an impartial perspective may have helped. There can often be political and/or emotional bias.

The benefits of autobiography is that it can reflect the feelings and impressions of the author and often convey emotions that are otherwise lost. Autobiography is also a product of its time and autobiographies written in reflection can contrast with those written in the immediacy of the situation. They may also reflect the political and social mores of the time.

Romulus, My Father is autobiographical in nature but the main focus of the text is on the personal journey of the composer's father and is , therefore, biographical. Gaita spends some time discussing personal details about himself and his family. This builds an overall picture of his life while he recounts that of his father. It gives the audience a fuller picture of Raimond Gaita's life on a personal and emotional level even though the text is primarily about Romulus Gaita.

Also, adding to the sense of the writing being very personal are the vivid scenes and descriptions that show the unusual characters in their lives and also set in an alien landscape - the country. These scenes reveal much about the inner workings of the author's mind and the philosophical background to how Raimond views the world and events surrounding his father and mother.

The value of this text lies not just in the life story told but the hope and moral truths that emerge. As you read the text look for the positives that Gaita, a writer and philosopher, takes from his father's life journey. The text highlights his philosophy of life and colours the way Gaita sees the world and himself. Gaita's changing life is shared in a manner that shows truths but also hides some. He mentions that he has changed names at the beginning of the text.

THE AUTHOR

Raimond Gaita is a German-born Australian philosopher and award-winning writer. He is a distinguished left wing academic who has held positions at both the Institute of Advanced Research at the Australian Catholic University and King's College, the University of London. Many of his past writings have been anti the Iraq war and the Howard Government and more recently he has opposed those that condone torture in defence against terrorism. These have been widely published and can be accessed on the Internet.

Romulus, My Father reveals insight into his philosophical ideas and approaches to the issues he has taught and studied. Gaita writes with a philosophical approach to his family's problems. This is reflected in how he deals with situations.

Gaita's life is best described in his own words and we get a sense of his identity from the language and revelations in the text. At times Gaita tells us as much about himself as he does about his father. This is in keeping with Couser's theory that memoir writing is about representations of identity. (*Memoir: An Introduction* by C. Thomas Couser, OUP, 2014)

Gaita has been married twice and has two children Katie and Eva. He has a strong body of published work including *Good and Evil: An Absolute Conception* and *A Common Humanity*.

CONTEXT

Background to World War Two

WWII is considered primarily a European war because it began when Germany, led by Adolf Hitler, attacked most of Europe. Beginning in Czechoslovakia and moving on to Poland, Norway, Denmark, Belgium and Holland in succession the Germans con-trolled most of Europe. Soon the world was involved in its most destructive, violent and wide-spread war in its history. Hitler was the Fascist leader in Germany and his policies affected all of the conquered countries in Europe and their inhabitants. Italy is a good example of these policies impacting the lives of the people.

Fascism

Italy at this time was under the control of the Fascist government of Mussolini and was involved in the war as an ally of Germany. Mussolini was dependent economically and militarily on Hitler. Although the early Fascist regime had not actively promoted anti-Semitism, Mussolini wished to keep Hitler's favour. The Fascist Race Manifestos (1938) declared that the Italians and the Aryans were dominant races, while there were a number of sub-human races including the Jews and Negroes. These Manifestos declared that Jews were forbidden to engage in certain professions or to marry non-Jews. The Star of David was to be worn as an identifying symbol. All Jewish people who had settled in Italy after 1919 had their citizenship revoked. Jewish refugees fleeing this persecution in other parts of Europe were interned in camps.

However, at this time, these camps were not like concentration camps and conditions in them were quite tolerable. There was no upsurge of anti-Semitic feeling within the general population as Jews were well-integrated and accepted. The main effect of the Manifestos was a lack of freedom and rights, and for some, incarceration.

In 1943, Mussolini fell from power and Italy did an about face, surrendering to the Allies. The Nazis re-occupied Northern Italy and conditions worsened for Italian Jews. A coded message from Berlin to Rome intercepted by the Allies at the time called for 'the immediate and thorough eradication of the Jews in Italy' as being in the interest of 'general security in Italy'. Supporters of Mussolini and the SS sought out and arrested many who were later transported to Auschwitz-Birkenau.

The Final Solution

In the latter years of the war, the Nazis implemented their 'final solution', a euphemism for systematic genocide. Supposedly inferior individuals were killed. These included Negroes, homosexuals, intellectually or physically disabled people, prisoners of conscience and Jews. It was the Jews who were principally targeted. The "selections" in the camp are a part of this 'final solution'.

The Camps

The Auschwitz-Birkenau camp was one of a large number of camps set up by the Nazis during World War II. The way in which all of these camps were organised was similar. The old, the young and the sick were usually killed as soon as they arrived at the camp or very soon afterwards. Of the rest, they were kept in conditions of such deprivation and forced to work so hard that exhaustion and illness soon took its toll.

Internment camps were administered by internees. They maintained their positions by brutality and were hated and feared by those underneath them. When the camps were liberated, many were murdered by their companions.

Immigration to Australia after WWII

The communist Russian forces overran many of the countries that were conquered by the Nazis by the end of the war. This was as bad, if not worse, than the fascist regime they replaced. Joseph Stalin who was a true dictator and murdered millions of his own people, ran the Russian government. Of course, many people wanted to flee the communists in countries such as Hungary, Czechoslovakia, Yugoslavia and others.

Many were tired of war and sought a new life in a new country and Australia was about as far away as you could get from Europe. The Nazis had shown that race hatred was ignorant and the prejudices that existed before the war were slowly disappearing. After the war immigration was seen as positive and governments stepped in to assist.

Firstly with Britain and then with other nations such as Holland, Italy, Yugoslavia and Greece the government paid for the refugee's passage in return for two years work with wages at a place directed by the government. This is the situation that Romulus found himself in with his wife and son. The government did this successfully for hundreds of thousands of migrants to Australia.

Racism in Australia after WWII

As already mentioned there was far more tolerance for 'foreigners' in Australia after the war but this mainly extended to 'white' immigrants. During the war Australians had worked with and fought against a whole array of nationalities and so some of the isolation was broken down.

There was still some racism against other groups or individuals. We see this in *Romulus, My Father* where we read of the words 'refo' and 'Balt' amongst others. On the whole Australia welcomed these individuals and their contribution to society.

PLOT OUTLINE

Romulus is born in Romania

Escapes to Yugoslavia and is an apprentice blacksmith

Moves to Germany then war breaks out

Falls in love with Christine, a German girl and they marry

Raimond is born

Christine begins to show signs of mental illness and asthma

They move to Australia for her asthma

Romulus moves to the camps and the family to Baringhup

Christine has affair with Mitru, one of many affairs she conducted.

Christine and Mitru move to Melbourne

Christine returns intermittently

Raimond is returned to his father as his mother can't care for him

Romulus has accident on motorbike

Raimond has mini-rebellion

Christine and Mitru have huge problems

Mitru suicides ——— Christine declines
mentally and
Romulus can't help

Christine suicides ———

Romulus falls in love
with Lydia

Romulus finds out
Lydia has lied to him
and is married

Susan and Barbara
are adopted out and
Hora is saddened

Romulus has mental
health problems

Raimond visits him in
the psychiatric
hospital

Romulus recovers to
a level where he can
exist

Romulus meets and
marries Milka

They live happily
but childless in
Maryborough

Raimond finds Susan
and Barbara and the
family are reunited

Romulus becomes ill
and goes to hospital

Romulus dies and
Raimond gives a
moving eulogy

SUMMARY

chapter one

Gaita's family story begins with an image of violence. Romulus stands with a pitchfork to fend off his drunken uncle. He jumps out the window goes to his mother's and leaves for Yugoslavia at age thirteen.

This dramatic start sets the scene of Gaita's tale of his father's life journey and to some extent his family's and his own. Romulus was born in Markovic, Romania in 1922 and his upbringing was difficult as his father died when he was an infant. The family was poor and Romulus had to work hard to maintain a basic standard of living.

Romulus went to school and loved education, especially reading. He often read Bible stories and these gave him a lifelong religious spirituality. Unfortunately school only lasted four years and he missed a scholarship as his application was late.

In 1935 Romulus ran away. He managed to travel one hundred and fifty kilometres and secured an apprenticeship as a blacksmith. It was an extremely hard life and work went from 1 am to 4 pm. With no pay he did extra work to earn money which he used to clothe himself. He excelled at blacksmithing and was so good he took time out to read.

When the apprenticeship finished he left and went to Germany to work. During the war he was conscripted by the Germans. Sent to Dortmund in 1944 he met sixteen year old Christine Anna Dorr with whom he fell in love. Christine was very attractive to men and was well educated.

Romulus was also now a handsome man, although he called himself a gypsy as his skin was so dark. By 1944 he was involved in the black market and had access to things which were strictly rationed. It is interesting to note that Gaita writes if they,

'had been discovered together by the Gestapo they would almost certainly have been shot, victims of Nazi racial policy' (p7)

In this situation they met secretively and Raimond was conceived in a cemetery. Due to the circumstances of the war it was a very intense relationship. They fought and Christine was jealous. Romulus once tried to shoot himself when she left him but things seem to settle at the end of the war.

After Raimond was born she changed and began to show the signs of mental illness that would haunt her for the remainder of her life. She was incapable of caring for the baby but the family helped and the baby was well looked after. Romulus gains a good job that he likes doing iron work but Christine has asthma and wants to move. She chooses Australia where her illness was supposed to improve.

They head to Australia in 1950 with an assisted passage on the S.S. Hersey.

Questions for chapter one

- In five lines describe Romulus' childhood.

- How is his life as an apprentice presented to the reader?

- How is Christine described? Discuss how the interactions between the two are made complex by Christine's mental illness.

- Research the concept of 'assisted passage' to post war Australia

Present your findings as a report.

- Why do you think the two prophecies are mentioned in this chapter? What effect do these prophecies have on both the reader and Romulus and Christine? Do you think these foreshadowings affect the way Christine and Romulus see the world and each other?

chapter two

The family arrived in Port Melbourne in April 1950. They were then sent to a migrant camp and on to Baringhup in central Victoria. The job for Romulus was building a dam and families weren't allowed to live on site so the family stayed in town.

Baringhup was a central Victorian village on the Loddon River and was well past its 'heyday' which was in the late 1800s. When the Gaitas arrive it is a much smaller town and the men living in the camps preferred the larger towns of Maldon, Maryborough or Castlemaine for nights out. One way of getting to Maldon was by Keith and Myra Laity's taxi run. These business owners befriended Romulus.

Gaia then muses on the Australian landscape and its desolation in European eyes. Romulus' first Romanian friends in Australia were two brothers, Pantelimon (Hora) and Dumitru (Mitru) Hora. The brothers had fled the communists, travelled to Italy and then to Australia. They were both good looking men who became close friends. Hora became an especially valued friend.

The jobs the migrant men were given were menial compared to their skills but Romulus focussed on finishing his two years of work and then making a life for himself. Raimond writes that he 'rarely' saw his father during this period but the tension between his mother and father was evident. His mother was very promiscuous and let Raimond run wild.

Because of this, Raimond was allowed to live with his father at the camp for a month and when his father was on shift work Hora cared for him. This went on too long and the camp authorities wanted the child gone. The situation 'drifted' on and Romulus' strain grew. He smacks Raimond for lying about the aftershave he took and Hora has to intervene.

Raimond's mother comes to visit and he has time with her at the river and in the countryside. Soon they move to a farmhouse called Frogmore that they share with a Ukrainian couple.

Questions for chapter two

- Why is the family moved to Buringhup?

- Why do you think that Romulus asks for other Romanians when he gets to camp? In your response think about cultural interaction.

- How do the European immigrants find the Australian landscape?

- Describe Raimond's mother's behaviour.

- Why does the family move to the farmhouse?

- What qualities, both positive and negative, do we learn about Romulus in this chapter?

You can present your response in table form like the sample below.

Romulus' Qualities

Positive	Negative

chapter three

Frogmore was in a dilapidated condition but it was on one hundred and sixty acres. Small and without any luxuries such as electricity or running water, it also had rats, which bit them in their beds. The peppercorn trees around the house were there 'to mediate between European and local landscapes'. (p23) It was so isolated and quiet that they could hear the noise from the dam building four kilometres away.

After a couple of months the Ukrainians moved and the Gaitas have the house to themselves and two dogs. The house was extremely 'primitive' and his mother had no idea how to manage it. She could not settle and was bored and lonely. It is here that she first begins her affair with Mitru and they spend much time together.

The work finishes for Romulus and he gets a new job at the tool factory in Maryborough while the brothers went to the salt works in Werribee. Hora then comes back to work at the tool works and Mitru gets a job in Melbourne at the railway's lost property office. Christine leaves Frogmore to live with him with Raimond who also becomes fond of Mitru. Christine is very promiscuous and has many lovers, causing much grief. She also wastes money. Young Raimond roams the streets and begins to beg for money. Once caught he is reprimanded by the police and it is decided he would be better off with his father. His father now has two motorbikes, a Bantam and a Sunbeam. He works two jobs and has long hours.

Raimond then relates two incidents that help define his father and the migrant experience to some extent. The first is when he nearly causes a bushfire by setting fire to a haystack to kill a snake. He was even ridiculed as a 'New Australian for his folly.'

Romulus was mortified by this incident but he makes up for it in the second incident when he saves the life of Neil Mikkelsen when he falls off a ladder.

As Romulus had to do shift work, Raimond was often left alone at the farmhouse and he found this frightening. He tells of once fleeing the house with his mother and then running from Hora who was coming home from work. Raimond takes the dogs to bed with him.

When his mother comes to visit she is depressed and can't care for him. Romulus works overtime but can't rely on her to care for their son. Christine was a lonely woman and only Neil Mikkelson talked to her . The others are hostile as she is a neglectful mother. Mikkelson remembers her fondly years later as a 'woman of substance'.

One night she takes an overdose of sleeping tablets and is taken to hospital to have her stomach pumped. Back at Frogmore after this she is distant and spends much of her time in bed. Another night she disappears and an unsuccessful search is conducted by the community. Christine returns the next morning and says she slept in the bush.

Her behaviour becomes more erratic and she often spends all day in bed. She complains about Romulus to others but these complaints have no foundation. Soon she returns to Melbourne to live with Mitru. Raymond writes them both letters.

Questions for chapter three

- What do the peppercorn trees signify?

- In your own words describe Frogmore.

- Why are there problems between Christine and Mitru? What external influences are there on the interactions they have?

- How does Raimond become involved with the police?

- Choose one incident involving Romulus and state carefully what it says about him and his adopted country. In your response think about conflicting cultures and beliefs.

- Create a list of Christine's erratic behaviour.

- What effects does this erratic behaviour have on Raimond?

- Why do you think Christine returns to Melbourne to live with Mitru?

chapter four

After Christine goes to Melbourne Raimond settles in with his father and four animals. They are:

- Rusha the cow
- Marta the cat
- Orloff the dog
- Jack the cockatoo

Jack was the most important and he lives free and sleeps on the door. Jack liked the Jack Benny quiz show on the radio and was excited by it. This excitement led to him eating through the wall.

Marta was a feral cat and she used to be bitten by Jack. She gave birth to five kittens, one of which was Billy the tom cat. He and Jack used to play together and Jack never pecked him. Jack was intensely loyal to Romulus and the affection was returned, especially when Jack came into the house in the mornings.

Jack went to the school with Raimond, sometimes flying, sometimes on the handlebars of the bike. During the day he would fly around Buringhup and create mischief. Romulus had to clip his wing because Jack was threatened with death. One time he beheaded all Miss Collard's flowers and had to walk back in the rain. One day Jack gave them all a shock by laying an egg in Romulus' bed. The egg never hatched.

Orloff gave Raimond a sense of security although the dog lacked any intelligence. Jack used to whistle him and he would come although Jack mocked him. Orloff survived a shooting for sheep chasing but was poisoned later. The Gaita's cried for him and Raimond thought his 'chest would explode with grief.'

Rusha the cow was always escaping but had 'fine calves' and 'had it in' for Raimond. She nearly killed him once at the wall of the dam.

Romulus started a poultry farm when he lost his job at the tool factory. He began with a thousand hens and they 'roamed free'. They had to wash the eggs and Romulus designs and builds an egg washing machine that was two person operated.

In winter during 1954 both Christine and Mitru came to live at Frogmore but they quarrelled with each other and with Romulus. Mitru leaves and Romulus wonders why he has these problems. On returning from taking Mitru to the station he crashes his motorbike and breaks his leg. Christine and Raimond go to see him at the hospital and she is remorseful as she feels she is to blame. Mitru returns to help until Hora arrives to look after the chooks.

Hora came to help but he didn't like or respect Christine as she was lazy. Hora did everything and he tried to give Raimond oranges but Christine kept eating them. The oranges were hard to get to Frogmore and Hora eventually argued with Christine about them. Hora was also worried about the hens at this time as they were dying. He couldn't kill them so he buried them alive.

None of this helped his patience and the relationship he had with Christine was hostile. Hora only respected Romulus and it was his word that counted. One day Christine baited Hora and he threatened to beat her if she stayed so she left for Melbourne, eventually again living with Mitru.

After she goes things settle down and Hora cares for Raimond in loco parentis. They work together on the eggs and Raimond spends the money he earns on comics. This goes on for months until Romulus comes home from the hospital. Raimond notes that Jack was delighted to see Romulus again. Hora soon moves out to Maryborough where he lives at the back of an Italian Wine Bar.

Things continue at Frogmore and Raimond points out that his father hated lying and relates an anecdote that describes this. He takes one of Romulus' most treasured possessions, a razor, and destroys the blade. To cover up he throws it in the dam. His father suspects he is responsible for it and says to him to tell the truth about it. Raimond lies and Romulus knows it and smacks him. Hora has to intervene so that Raimond can escape. He never tells what happened to the razor.

Frogmore had deteriorated and the house was literally falling apart. It gave them little protection from the elements. They had a one burner kerosene stove and their diet was very constant, eggs for breakfast with a variation on potato soup for dinner.

Romulus decides to stop poultry farming and start blacksmithing again. He uses the blacksmithing shop at Tom Lille's. He enjoys working at his trade but things are still hard. Fruit is the one thing that Raimond can eat at will and Romulus buys it by the caseload. While they were poor, Raimond had more than Romulus as a child and they 'were in need of nothing'. All they didn't have was a car.

Raimond looked forward to the treats he got at Lillie's when he was there for morning or afternoon tea on occasions. The sisters, Mrs Lillie and Miss Collard were old and forgetful but kind. They were good to Raimond and an anecdote reveals Miss Collard's sense of humour.

Questions for chapter four

- Describe one of the animals at Frogmore and its characteristics. Use a quote from the text.

- How does Romulus crash the motorbike?

- Why do Hora and Christine dislike each other?

- What does the incident of the razor show about both Raimond and Romulus? What effect do morals and ethics have on interactions with people and the way a character sees the world?

- What is happening to the house at Frogmore?

- Why does Romulus return to blacksmithing?

- Why do you think Raimond includes the last anecdote about Miss Collard?

chapter five

Raimond likes both Mrs Collard and Mrs Lillie but he often sat up with Miss Lillie. Both women felt pity for him because of his mother and they often wanted to help. Romulus was worried that Raimond would get wild without a woman's hand.

One incident occurred when Raimond was eleven and he became involved with a wild family who had a poor reputation. The eldest daughter taught him about Elvis Presley. He went home and created a scrapbook defending Elvis and left it for his father to find. Romulus tore it up and questions Raymond.

Romulus believed that children should be respectful but had no interest in social status. Raimond does little work around the place and Tom Lillie thinks he is lazy. Raimond prefers to read but one day he thinks he should be like other boys and shoot rabbits. He goes up into the hills but only notices the beauty of the landscape and decides he can't kill. He returns home to find his father crazy with worry.

Raimond is very interested in books and is encouraged by Ronald Mottek, a primary teacher at the local school. He encouraged Raimond to learn and while his teaching was 'unconventional' it was sound. Mottek and Romulus had a respect for each other and Mottek warns Raimond to behave so 'the disappointment' wouldn't kill Romulus.

At weekends they visited friends or went to the very primitive cinema. They travelled everywhere on the motorbike and Raimond sat on the petrol tank until he was eight years old. They dressed for warmth and Raimond was embarrassed as he had newspapers as insulation on his chest. The motorbike was a Sunbeam bought from a Lithuanian man, Vacek.

Vacek later suffered poor mental health and lived between two boulders outside Maldon sealed with corrugated iron. He cooked, sometimes in his own urine, and occasionally spent time in a mental hospital. He sometimes stayed with the Gaitas and he came and went as he pleased. Vacek was well educated and he had a 'poetic, dreamy nature'. He had a 'communion' with animals and he also had 'open hearted' feelings for people.

Summers at Frogmore were hot and Hora loved to sunbake. They often swam in the dam or at Cairn Curran. Hora built a diving board in the dam which led him to teach Raimond to swim. He did this by tying a rope to his waist tied to the pole. When Raimond sank he pulled him up. He managed to learn dog paddle and he then shared Hora's love of water.

Later Hora and Romulus built a boat and Romulus and Vacek wouldn't go in it because they didn't like the water. Once Raimond and Hora tried to swim across Cairn Curran, unsuccessfully. Another day they have to swim. They tow the boat to shore and walk six kilometres back to Frogmore. They were so late Romulus had rung the police.

When they sailed Hora told him stories, first adventure tales and then stories of great men such as Albert Schweitzer, Isaac Semmelweis and Bertrand Russell. From Hora and Romulus' conversations Raimond learns about individuality and character. They were open 'to the voices of others' (p.73) and he is affected by books such as Solzhenitsyn's *The Gulag Archipelago*. This book teaches him that people are corrupted by compromises and this shook him for years, 'his understanding of himself seriously altered'. This is a good example of how explorations into literature and interacting with books can lead to profound enlightenments and personal change. Raimond learns a lot about life from books as well as his father and Hora.

Questions for chapter five

- How does Raimond rebel?

- Why is Romulus angry at him for this?

- How is Ronald Mattek presented?

- Describe either Romulus' or Raimond's clothing when they ride the motorbike.

- Who is Vacek and how does he come into contact with the Gaitas?

- In your own words describe one adventure or incident they have on the boat.

- Research Alexander Solzhenitsyn's work *The Gulag Archipelago*.

- What is it about and what impact did it have on the young Raimond?

- What does Raimond learn from Romulus and Hora?

chapter six

Raimond goes to Melbourne in the summer of 1954 to have holidays with Mitru and Christine. They fail, however, to meet him at Spencer St Station and the stationmaster calls the police. Raimond spends the night at the station. Mitru and Christine get him in the morning and they head to his mother's flat at Burnley.

Christine suffered badly from asthma and she often gasped for breath even with her spray. She also heard voices and had undergone, unsuccessfully, electric shock treatment. She was hospitalised and Raimond went back to Frogmore. On his return he carries a 'confession' from Mitru to Romulus. Mitru wants Romulus to divorce Christine and you can see the respect he has for Romulus in the letters. Mitru was grateful for Romulus' generosity and strength of character.

Romulus in turn was 'fond' of Mitru but not as much as he was of Hora. He never blamed Mitru for the affair but pitied him. He blamed Christine, 'She was a woman who liked men' (p.83) Romulus wouldn't get a divorce because he didn't believe in it. Occasionally Christine would come to stay and perhaps a 'reconciliation' may have been discussed. She even tried to be a mother but still had hallucinations and heard voices.

Raimond's mother left soon after to live with Mitru. Less than two months later she gave birth to a daughter, Susan. They lived at the back of a wine saloon owned by Mr and Mrs Foschia. The bar was patronised by immigrants but also some Australian drunks. Mrs Foschia was tougher than her husband and stopped him giving away free drinks and ran the house strictly.

Christine soon began to neglect Susan and wouldn't change her nappies. She and Mitru quarrelled over Susan and Mitru got a second job because the rent was in arrears. Christine still flirted with the young men in the boarding house. Romulus pays the rent but he tells Mitru that the Foschias' have no tolerance for him and Christine. He hits Romulus. Mitru then cries and apologises but the situation between him and Christine is desperate. Mitru tries to stab himself to death but fails and has to promise the police he will not attempt suicide again.

The tension and quarrelling continue, Hora is worried and he tells Mitru to, 'get his act together'. He tells Mitru to leave Christine. On a summer night in 1956 Mitru comes to Frogmore with Susan and they all try to put events behind them. Raimond even goes to stay with Mitru and Christine later at the wine bar but Christine is worse and Mitru beats her. They reconcile but a week later he beats her again because she neglects Susan. He takes Susan for a walk and returns an hour later.

Mitru then leaves and jumps to his death. Christine is again pregnant, three months at that stage. Christine thinks about following him and jumping but goes back to Frogmore. The Catholics refused to bury Mitru but the Anglican priest agreed. He is buried and no-one ever knew why he suicided. Various reasons are given and it seems he choose to die rather than 'compound the guilt, the shame and the misery.' (p.93)

Questions for chapter six

- Why isn't Raimond picked up at the station?

- What is asthma? Describe its effects. How might physical illness affect the way an individual sees the world and interacts with it?

- Would Mitru's letters have affected you if you were Romulus? Describe your reaction to them. Discuss letters as a form of interaction.

- Describe either Mr or Mrs Foschia. How do they see the world and one specific character?

- How does Christine treat Susan? Give a specific example. Why can't she relate to her own child?

- Why does Mitru hit Romulus? Violence is another form of interaction. How is it described in the text?

- Why won't the Catholic priest bury Mitru?

- List the suspected reasons for Mitru's suicide.

chapter seven

After Mitru's death Romulus is preoccupied and troubled. Raimond tells his father that he thinks he doesn't love him but this causes him much regret when Romulus has an accident on the motorbike. He has been badly injured and has a tube in his mouth when they see him in the hospital. He recovers and goes back to working long hours as a blacksmith. Here he was happiest and was a very skilled workman, but his skill was not confined to metal. He makes clothes, shoes, spins wool and carves bone. He can repair anything.

His skill shows Raimond 'the relation between work and character' (p.98) and how honesty is the mark of our humanity. His reputation as an excellent tradesman spread and he did well. Raimond then discusses how his good name was important because migrants were tolerated not respected. Both Romulus and Hora 'appreciated' this tolerance. It is interesting that they both ignored the 'external signs of status and prestige' (p.101). Character was an important concept for them and this differed from the concept of 'personality'.

In Australian eyes Christine had no character and did not fit the 'deadening attractions of middle class respectability'. (p.103) Raimond discusses, in depth, the 'contempt' people had for her and how she could not escape her own limitations.

In 1957 Romulus starts writing to Lydia, a Yugoslav woman who is very young and attractive. The relationship becomes serious and they seem to have fallen in love. There was even talk of marriage. Raimond is now allowed to ride the motorbike and he collects the letters from the post office. This gives him a real sense of freedom.

Questions for chapter seven

- Why do you think Romulus is preoccupied with Mitru's death?

- Romulus is happy blacksmithing. Why is this so?

- What other skills does Romulus have?

- How are migrants perceived in this period of Australian history according to Gaita? Do some research in this area and see if his opinions match other opinions and the facts.

- Do you agree with society's view of Christine or do you think she is misunderstood? Support your ideas with examples and quotes from the text.

- Who is Lydia? Discuss her interaction with Romulus and her lack of a moral and ethical basis.

- Why is Raimond allowed to ride the motorbike?

chapter eight

Raimond heads to St Patrick's College in Ballarat at the start of 1958 as his father thinks it is a good school. He hasn't heard from his mother since the funeral of Mitru. Susan and the new baby, Barbara, were in homes and they were made wards of the state in 1957. Christine became a day patient at a psychiatric centre and she goes to visit Raimond one day at school.

His mother takes him for lunch and embarrasses him and then tells him of her past with her father. She regrets what has happened and this leaves Raimond 'disturbed' and 'resentful'. She then tries to get back with Romulus but this never occurs. She kills herself by taking an overdose of sleeping tablets and drowning in her own vomit. The Catholics bury her because the death certificate says asphyxiation. Romulus always loved her and writes to explain the death.

Raimond, his father and Hora never appreciated 'the degree to which my mother's life and behaviour were affected by her psychological illness.' (p.112) She was profoundly ill and no one seemed to realise it. Christine was a point of contention between Raimond and his father for ages until it was finally settled in 1981 when they built her a headstone.

Questions for chapter eight

- Why does Raimond go to St Patrick's?

- What happens to Susan and Barbara?

- Why does Christine visit Raimond? What happens in this incident? Discuss their interactions and the factors that affect them.

- How does his mother die?

- How do both father and son resolve their differences over her?

- It is interesting to research mental illness in Australia during the 1950s and 1960s. It will give you an insight into how Christine and later Romulus were treated and how difficult it was for people such as them. Consider how interactions with mentally ill people in society have changed.

chapter nine

Romulus and Hora were concerned about the girls, Susan and Barbara. They both tried to adopt them and Hora visited often. Unfortunately, the girls were adopted out because Romulus didn't maintain his contact as 'he was falling into insanity' (p.117) He found out from a woman who knows Lydia that Lydia is not the woman he thought she was and he suffers badly after this realisation.

On writing to Lydia he learns that she is already married and he becomes confused, wondering why she had done it to him. It seemed to destroy his moral world and he could not comprehend her betrayal. Raimond likens his loss to the 'Prayer for the Dead' in *The Book of Common Prayer,*

> *'Man that is born of woman hath but a short time to live and is full of misery. He cometh up and is cut down like a flower. He fleeth as it were a shadow and never continueth in one stay.'*

He admits himself into Ballarat Psychiatric Hospital in September 1960 and Raimond visits him. It was disturbing as Romulus was bewildered and dosed up on Largactil. Romulus was ambivalent about his visit and he claimed he was not really ill. His father's illness colours Raimond's life for a time and Romulus tries to hide his insanity to protect his son but it manifests itself in aberrant behaviour.

Romulus begins to see things, believe in superstitious things and see signs in the slightest behaviours. He once tries to overdose but Tom Lillie saves him. His passionate nature became passionate madness. To get him into hospital Raimond promises to deliver his furniture to the stores for Christmas.

Raimond calls up John Dunstan, a school friend, to help. He relates a short biography of Dunstan who later jumps to his death from a block of flats in Carlton. John thinks Frogmore is a dump but they get to work on moving all the tables and chairs. Raimond has learnt to drive the ute and this makes it easier.

John is terrified this first night by Vacek who comes out in the half light from a bedroom. When Vacek realises they don't need him to help he leaves. They get all the deliveries done and then have nothing to do. The two boys begin to drive around, even racing other locals and staying in Castlemaine. This adventure ends when the local policeman, Jack Matthey, follows up on a report of hooliganism and takes the car keys.

Months later he catches Raimond driving around and he charges Raimond and Romulus. In court he speaks for them and they are fined but no conviction is recorded because of what he says. When Romulus comes home from the hospital he is not cured but begins work. Romulus visits Raimond at school and he is shocked by his father's appearance at the school with an equally odd Vacek.

After this Romulus decides to go to Sydney to shoot the husband of Lydia, as they had just both arrived in Australia. Raimond then philosophises on passion and morality and how he couldn't condemn his father because of Lydia's 'cold blooded mendacity' (p.137) They go to Sydney together and politely wait until nine o'clock to knock on the door. Lydia opens it and she is beautiful and it is this beauty that saves her husband. They leave after a long conversation.

Romulus thinks of suicide on the way home but his shame pulls him out of his misery. This incident begins his healing and he seems to understand his affliction.

Questions on chapter nine

- How does Romulus find out about Lydia's lies?

- Describe the effect on Romulus of Lydia's deceit.

- How does Raimond feel when he sees his father in Ballarat Psychiatric Hospital?

- In your own words tell the story of John Dunstan.

- Compile a list of the symptoms Romulus exhibits.

- Describe how you would view the incident of Romulus going to Sydney to kill Lydia's husband if you were Raimond? Discuss the complex personal and moral interactions that occur in this incident.

chapter ten

During his illness Romulus quarrels with his friends and workers. He has an incident with Stan Smolek where he refuses to work and in another incident, Vacek leaves him forever. Vacek then goes on to become institutionalised and stays in for the rest of his life. He also quarrels with Hora very badly over Susan and Barbara.

Hora was annoyed that he had signed the girls over to the authorities and it was worse because he wasn't able to see them again. Hora is reunited with them thirty years later when Raimond tracks them down. Hora and Romulus stay friends but lead separate lives.

Romulus' mental illness leads him to be deluded in how he sees his conversations with others and this self-deception was contrary to how he lived his life based on truth.

In 1962 Raimond convinces his father to buy a house in Maryborough because the land he had bought for him and Lydia wouldn't ever have a house on it. He stays in this house until he dies. During this period he also pays for the passage of Lydia's mother and brother to Australia because he had promised. This is despite what Lydia had done to him.

They both came to live in the house in Maryborough and were kind to Raimond. The mother thought that Romulus might marry her and worked toward it. One night 'M' arrives and they have a party and get drunk. Lydia's mum sleeps with 'M' thinking it was Romulus and 'M' has to leave the next morning. She moves out to Sydney soon after.

Raimond is now almost sixteen and has a changed relationship with his father. He decides to leave St Patrick's after an incident over shoes but is talked into staying the year out. He still intends to leave and go to Melbourne High School. He wins the argument and goes to live in Melbourne.

Eventually Raimond moves into the same boarding house as Hora and here they have the only adult argument of their lives over communism. Hora decides he could not speak to Raimond of anything that mattered because of his support for the unions and their communist leaders. He literally had nothing to say to Raimond.

Questions for chapter ten

- Why does Vacek leave? How might his mental state affect his interactions with others and the world?

- What happens to Vacek after this?

- What happens to Susan and Barbara?

- Why does Romulus pay for Lydia's mother and brother to come to Australia?

- Why does Lydia's mother leave the Maryborough house?

- Why does Hora stop talking to Raimond? Why might not interacting be effective on occasion?

chapter eleven

This chapter outlines how Romulus and Milka came to be married. It comes through an arranged meeting and twenty-nine year old Milka was 'just right' for Romulus. They agree to live together for a trial period and this must have been hard for Milka because Romulus was unstable. Milka, however, was his equal in arguments and she was financially independent and they were married in six months. They built a workshop together as they needed it when Tom Lillie died and his daughter leased the farm. They built it together and worked long hours.

Raimond recalls his father's compassion and generosity. He received little thanks for bringing many people, including the uncle from whom he fled, to Australia. He also sent thousands of dollars to Yugoslavia. He lent money that was never repaid and got no thanks. He never worried about hypocrisy or ignorance.

In contrast to this he enjoyed the company of relatives and 'longed for European society'. He missed Hora who now had a family of his own but he loved Melbourne with its crowds and people. He even went back to Yugoslavia in 1981 after the communist rule collapsed but returned, appreciating Australia more.

In the 1960s and 1970s Romulus was 'more or less' better but he maintained his casual approach to dress and 'His affliction gave authority' to his words on moral issues. He liked to talk and enjoyed conversation very much. He had little respect for authority and self-importance.

His personality was complicated and his interactions with others were unusual at times. People were often bemused by his actions. After his illness he had no time for the superficial. Raimond notes that he had a complicated relationship with his father and they quarrelled often. One Christmas Raimond drove to Melbourne, only to return to Maryborough immediately.

He stated that his father 'was out of touch with reality' and both his strength of character and his relationship with Milka helped stabilise him. Raimond got on well with Milka. It was a matter of regret that they couldn't have children and they tried to adopt.

Questions for chapter eleven

- Describe Milka.

- Construct a timeline of the events in the relationship between Romulus and Milka

- Create a list of examples of Romulus' good nature. How does this reflect on him as an individual? How might this impact his relationships?

- How did Romulus find Yugoslavia on his visit?

- How did his mental problems affect him during this period?

- Why do you think Raimond's relationship with his father became so complex? What did Raimond think of Milka?

chapter twelve

This chapter begins with Romulus talking to a group of hippies he met when his cows broke into their property. He refers to his superstitions with them but they 'no longer tormented him' (p.182) and he could study the stars without fear. He had a newfound respect in the community because 'attitudes to New Australians had changed.' (p.183)

Romulus had, by now, retired and he spent time growing vegetables or caring for the animals on his Carisbrook land. He had grown disillusioned with business in the 1980s and had given it up. He and Milka had lots of cows which they had to sell in the drought. They also kept goats.

One day Romulus collapsed with pain in his chest and left arm but the doctor said he was just dehydrated. His home became a menagerie and his Maryborough home always had animals in it. He even kept and cared for bees. They had left Jack the cockatoo at Frogmore hoping his wing would grow and he would fly away. Jack, of course, stayed.

Many people wondered at his sentimental attitude towards animals. He could, however, eat them to survive. Raimond's daughter, Eva, worried that he killed animals but she became accustomed to it. Romulus loved his animals.

Romulus and Milka survive on the pension and they are quite self-sufficient. Romulus no longer makes money from iron work and he even grows his own tobacco to make ends meet. It is unsmokable. During the period of the early to mid-1980s Raimond is urged by his father to search for Susan and Barbara but initially he had little interest. His interest in his extended family is aroused when he met his mother's sister in Germany.

He finds his half-sisters still alive in Melbourne and Wodonga. They are reunited in the mid-1980s. This was very important to his father who thought it helped restore the order of things. The girls had married and led normal lives with children of their own. This was also important to Romulus as it showed they weren't too damaged from their childhood.

Stopping the ironwork was not good for a man who was used to work and he had to create work for himself. Without work he became depressed and missed visitors, especially Hora who found it difficult to drive because of advancing arthritis. Romulus also missed Raimond who moved to England. Romulus took pride in Raimond's success but thinks his life is restless and is anxious about it.

Milka also felt this isolation and 'complained of it'. It was Romulus' fault because he took people at their word and couldn't accept a missed visit or lateness of any kind. He thought statements were promises. He declined faster with heart disease and in a few years was barely able to walk. He also refused to have an operation but finally agreed to a heart bypass.

The operation was a success but Romulus had a stroke which left him paralysed on one side and with memory problems. Raimond's wife, Yael, cared for him in hospital but he really looked forward to seeing Milka who mostly remained in Maryborough because of the animals. He partly recovered but then had another stroke while having an angiogram. After this he felt useless as he couldn't drive or see from one eye. He said,

'I am good for nothing. Just for the rubbish heap' (p.200)

Questions for chapter twelve

- How do the hippies treat Romulus? What does Raimond say about how they see his father?

- Why do Romulus and Milka have so many animals?

- How does he feel about finding both Susan and Barbara? Why is this important in the larger scheme of things?

- What is a heart attack?

- What is a stroke?

- Read the chapter carefully and note all the references to doctors. What is the author's tone? Do you think the author paints them in a negative or positive light? Support your answer with references to the text and comment on how these interactions are portrayed.

chapter thirteen

In May 1996 Romulus suffers pains and the doctor tells him it is indigestion. Milka rings the doctor again and is reassured but the next day she takes him again to the doctor and insists he goes to hospital. She rings Raimond and he finds out that his father has a 'dead gut' and has only twenty- four hours to live.

They all go to visit him and he is in intensive care and looks very bad. Hora is with him as well. He refuses to acknowledge the pain to Raimond. After Hora and Milka leave, Yael, Raimond's wife and his two daughters, Katie and Eva, come to visit. He sings a song with them and then never speaks again.

When they leave, Raimond stays until his father dies at 'just past midnight' and he calls Milka and then joins his family at the motel. The next day they organise the funeral and in the European tradition they have an open coffin. Romulus was buried on a Monday and Raimond gives the eulogy which was a summary of the book, *Romulus, My Father.* After the service he sees an elderly Australian man and it was Neil Mikkelsen who says to him,

'Every word you spoke was true...Your father saved my life.' (p.208)

Questions for chapter thirteen

- Why do you think the doctors treated Romulus with little regard? What does this tell us about bias and prejudice in interactions?

- Why do you think he tells the nurse anecdote?

- How does the story of the editor being out chasing 'mountain lions' affect Raimond?

- Why do you think Raimond left much from the eulogy?

- Compose an essay where you decide if Romulus was 'truly a man who would rather suffer evil than do it' in respect of his interactions with others and the world. Refer closely to the text.

SETTING

Yugoslavia

Yugoslavia was comprised of only two states, Montenegro and Serbia. During the period that is mentioned in the text it was a loose confederation of states that were united in 1918. After the Second World War it was named the Republic of Yugoslavia and united under communism with Josip Broz Tito as leader. Tito ruled the country as President from 1953 to 1980. The states that came together under this new Yugoslavia were-

- Bosnia and Herzegina
- Croatia
- Macedonia
- Slovenia
- Montenegro
- Serbia

This was home to nearly twenty million people. The country has long been split with ethnic divides and civil war. This seems to be ongoing and has caused many refugees to flee to new lands as many did to escape the communists after the war.

Yugoslavia is bordered by Romania, Hungary, Greece and Albania and true to its diverse nature has many ethnic groups and diverse religions with the main ones being Serbian Orthodox, Roman Catholic, Christian and Muslim.

Romania

Romania, a country formed in 1862, has undergone many transformations as the face of Europe has changed over the centuries. The most striking of these was the communist takeover in 1944 when Soviet forces marched in. The monarchy that had long ruled was abolished and a People's Republic was declared. This caused much social upheaval and many escaped the communists.

The communist regime was finally overthrown in 1989 with the end of the dictator, Nicolae Ceausescu. A new constitution was drawn and a democratic system introduced.

This European nation bordered both the Soviet Union before its disintegration and also the old Yugoslavia. Its near neighbours now are Bulgaria, Serbia, Hungary, Moldovia and the Ukraine. It has a sea border onto the Black Sea and its capital is Bucharest.

While Romanian is the official language others such as French, Hungarian and German are also widely used and this is alluded to in the text. Interestingly two percent of the population is classed as gypsy and this is also alluded to in the text.

Maryborough, Victoria

Victoria is a southern state of Australia with a population, in 2000, two years after the text was first published, of four and a half million people. Originally settled in 1835 it separated from NSW in 1851 and expanded due to the gold rush period. The capital is Melbourne and it has a strong agricultural background that is alluded to in the text when Romulus works on the Lillie farm.

Maryborough is a town north west of Ballarat with Maldon to the east of it. Both places are away from the coast and are rural rather than industrial towns. They are both within easy driving distance of the capital.

The house in Maryborough was bought at Raimond's instigation. It then served as the family home for the rest of Romulus' life. It is described as a 'modest weatherboard house' (p.148) but it also becomes a central point for much of the action, including Lydia's mother and brother's stay and the introduction of Milka to the reader. The house has many animals associated with it and Romulus also has a large vegetable garden.

Other places in Victoria are mentioned such as Ballarat and you should use an atlas to familiarise yourself with the general area if you have no first-hand experience of it. Try to get the sense of distance for a new migrant who came here just after the war and who had no experience with such vast spaces. This may help you understand how Christine is affected by the isolation and how Romulus also longs for the landscape and village life of Europe.

Frogmore

Frogmore is one of the main settings in the story and much of the text is centred here before Romulus moves into the town of Maryborough. It is the first house the Gaita family have and it is very primitive, having no running water or electricity. It is also very tiny being only seven and a half square metres with two bedrooms, a living room and a kitchen.

Raimond describes it very clearly,

> 'Verandahs ran along three sides and on one side there was a washhouse that doubled as a bathroom until a storm blew it away...The verandah wall at the front carried the name 'Frogmore' in raised cement letters painted green. A small bluestone dairy stood to the side of the house.' (p.22)

Among its other faults the house had rats living underneath that bit them in their beds at night. Soon the snakes followed the rats. Frogmore also had a dam that served a useful purpose in summer and Hora built a diving board into it.

Much of the plot centres on the house and the surrounding countryside. The dwelling is within walking distance of the Cairn Curran Reservoir that Romulus helped construct. Romulus even runs a poultry farm at Frogmore and they have a menagerie of animals.

During the course of their lives Frogmore deteriorates even more and conditions become very difficult as Raimond notes,

'Some of the joints under the floor in the hallway, the kitchen and the bedroom had given way and in those areas, the floor had sunk below the bottom of the skirting boards. The summers were hot and the house became unbearable, driving us to sleep on a mattress under the verandah.' (p.51)

The house served as a home for many of the characters in the book including Mitru, Hora, Christine and Vacek as well as Raimond and his father.

Jack

Setting Questions

- What shapes Romulus' early life including his time as an apprentice?

- Describe conditions in Germany during the war.

- Imagine you are Christine. In a diary entry describe how you find your new home after a week of being in Australia.

- Describe one incident where Romulus shows he is new to Australian culture.

- Describe Frogmore in your own words.

- How is the Australian countryside different from the European landscape?

- What does Romulus miss about his homeland?

- What does Romulus appreciate about Australia when he does return home?

CHARACTER ANALYSIS

Romulus

Romulus begins life in Romanian speaking Yugoslavia in 1922 but he always considered himself a Romanian. He ran away in 1935 and completed a blacksmithing apprenticeship. Moving to Germany he met and married Christine Anna Dorr, Raimond's mother.

Romulus by this time,

> *'had grown into a handsome man. He was dark but not tall, standing at 175 centimetres...His face was as open as his character. Everybody noticed his eyes, almond-shaped, hazel and intense... his nose was slightly askew...his features were soft and his mouth sensual. His body was...hard and muscular. (pp6-7)*

Romulus, after the war, moves to Australia for Christine's health where he is supposed to work for two years on the Cairn Curran Reservoir for the government. His relationship with Christine breaks down and she moves out with Mitru after trying to live at Frogmore. It is at Frogmore the author grew up with his father.

Romulus begins work at a variety of jobs and he saves the life of Neil Mikkelsen during this early period in the country. Christine becomes more erratic as her mental health worsens but Romulus can do little more than keep working. In 1954 he has the first of his motorbike accidents driving Mitru to the station after a quarrel. He recovers from this.

Through the text Raimond illustrates Romulus' philosophy of life and two good examples are the aftershave incident (p.18) and the razor incident (p.48). During the second Raimond writes,

*'I knew my father valued truthfulness above most things, and that
he would never willingly lie.' (p.50)*

After hospital Romulus returns to Frogmore and begins
blacksmithing at Lillie's. They have some friends in the area
who watch out for Raimond such as Miss Lillie. It is during this
period that Raimond 'offended his ideal of the respect owed by
children to their elders' (pp68-9) over the Elvis incident. Romulus
also earned respect from others such as Ronald Mottek, a local
teacher. Others in the local community came to respect him,
despite him being a migrant. Romulus has no sense of social
status and befriends all, including people such as Vacek.

Romulus has more domestic problems with Christine and Mitru
asks him to divorce her but he refuses. Romulus, 'didn't believe
in divorce' (p.83) This situation continues and Christine is now
pregnant and very unstable. After Mitru suicides Romulus helps
her but to no avail and she eventually suicides also. Romulus
continues his blacksmithing and his work shows his 'karacter'.
This concept was,

*'the central moral concept for my father...It stood for a settled
disposition for which it was possible rightly to admire someone.
(p.101)*

Romulus has two more serious relationships in his life after
Christine, one with Lydia by letter and one with Milka, whom
he marries. The relationship with Lydia is destroyed by her
'mendacity'. She has married another and used him. This leads
him to have a serious breakdown and become a psychiatric
patient. It takes him a long time to recover and even drives to
Sydney to kill her and her husband, but he just talks and leaves.

His mental deterioration and paranoia alienate his closest companions until even Hora is wary of him. Eventually, he recovers from Lydia's betrayal, and buys a house in Maryborough. He even fulfils his promise to bring Lydia's mother and brother to Australia and they live with him for a while.

The relationship with Milka was different and helped heal Romulus. Their meeting is arranged and they seem to get on and she tolerates his psychological eccentricities. She comes to live with him in Maryborough. They marry six months later and she stays with him until his death.

Through his time in Australia Romulus is always very generous with relatives and friends. This generosity is often abused but he still loves to have his relatives and friends around. He misses the European lifestyle. Raimond thinks this generosity was often misplaced,

'Compassion went unusually deep in my father. It showed itself all his life in the help he gave those in need and the pain he visibly felt for their pain...Whenever he made money...he looked to see who needed some.' (p.165)

While Romulus was 'pained' when people abused his generosity , he kept giving, even sending money back to Yugoslavia. He held strong his beliefs and this included his religion. Romulus always had a suspicion about organised religion but he always had,

'an instinctive reverence for the solemnity of church ritual and artefacts, even when he later became suspicious of institutional religion and prone to anti-clericalism' (p.3)

His spirituality was strong and he blended it with fatalism and his life experiences. As Romulus aged he recovered from his illness 'but he was permanently changed by it' (p.171). He cared little for appearance but maintained his love for intense conversation and would not talk about work outside hours but would gossip.

This intensity often stirred Raimond and he and his father fought, occasionally physically but Raimond got on well with Milka and this 'gratified' Romulus greatly. Romulus and Milka wanted children but couldn't have any and were refused adoption.

After Romulus retired from ironwork he cared for the animals but his health declined with heart problems. He eventually died of a gut related problem. Before he died he was pleased that Raimond found his half-sisters and that the damage of the early years had been repaired in some way,

> *'He believed that whatever might happen in the future, nothing could compromise the intrinsic good of our having found each other...He could not understand how anyone could prefer to live in ignorance or illusion about anything that mattered to the meaning of their lives.' (p.193)*

It is Raimond's eulogy for Romulus' that became the book. The words of his conclusion to this eulogy sum up his father's life and should be read closely (p.207). The final sentence is the most telling,

> *'He was truly a man who would suffer evil rather than do it'. (p.207)*

Questions for Romulus

- In your own words describe Romulus' early years at home and as an apprentice.

- How does Raimond detect the breakdown in his relationship with Christine?

- In one sentence sum up Romulus' life philosophy.

- Why do he and Hora get along so well?

- What does Lydia do that causes his breakdown?

- In what ways is his relationship with Milka unusual?

- Create a table that shows the positive and negative characteristics of Romulus. What overall impression of the man do you get from this table?

Raimond

We learn much about the life of Raimond from the narrative he gives about family life. To some extent *Romulus, My Father* is autobiographical in its content, especially about his early life. (For more information read the relevant section beginning on page 9). Some have described it as filial memoir and, as such, it represents more than one identity.

Raimond's own philosophy of life is clearly a reflection of his father's and he has gone on to become a scholarly philosopher. His early life can, in no way, be described as 'normal' in a suburban sense. With his mother unable to care for him his father seemed to understandably dominate and influence his life. In total his early life is male dominated and his father realises this. He was always welcoming female contact for Raimond such as time with Miss Lillie and Mrs Collard.

Romulus could be hard on Raimond at times when he was mischievous but generally, he was left to his own devices and he says his father 'asked little of me'. Tom Lillie thought he was lazy but Raimond,

'virtually had no interest in farm life, preferring to read.' (p.60)

It seems that it is on the farm at Frogmore the boy has a kind of philosophical epiphany,

'The landscape seemed to have a special beauty, disguised until I was ready for it,....It was as though God had taken me into the back of his workshop and shown me something really special... The experience transformed my sense of life and the countryside, adding to both a sense of transcendence' (p.61)

This philosophical take on life is advantageous to Raimond as he has many events in his life that are both dramatic and tragic. These include,

- His mother's suicide and mental disintegration
- Mitru's suicide
- Mitru beating his mother
- Romulus' mental breakdown
- Romulus' motorbike accidents
- The drive to Sydney to kill Lydia's husband

Raimond seems to emerge from these incidents with clear equanimity and this may be due to this philosophical outlook or the historical nature of the events he is recounting. At times he appears as the detached observer but at other times he is emotive, especially at times which involve his father. Two good examples of this are when he sees his father at the Ballarat Psychiatric Hospital and when he is dying.

Raimond has, as already mentioned, an unusual upbringing, being raised as a collective of Hora, Mitru, Christine, Vacek, Romulus and others. This does not seem to faze him or stop his education and we can tell from the language used in the text that he is well educated. He does highlight one teacher, Ronald Mottek, for special mention. These are significant interactions.

Romulus also seems to have a mind of his own from a young age and is quite independent, holding firmly to his beliefs. An example of this is when he wants to change schools because of the incident over the shoes. Raimond is also open to change as we see when he visits his father in the psychiatric hospital in Ballarat. Even here he is open to new ideas, feelings and experiences. For example in this situation we see,

'I left the hospital changed. I had absorbed past sorrows against the sure confidence of my father's strength. I knew that, whatever was to come, I could never do so again' (p.125)

Raimond supports his father through what is to come and does this without question even though they fight at times. Raimond's life is told through his father's and to some extent is a reflection of it. It is a remembrance that does justice to both. Thus, the structure or memoir form is one important way of exploring interactions in the sense of identity formation and the role others, especially parents, play in it.

Questions for Raimond

- Why would Raimond's upbringing be considered 'unconventional'?

- In one paragraph describe how you think Raimond sees his father:

  - Early in life
  - In his teenage years
  - As an adult
  - After his death

- Describe Raimond's philosophy of life.

- How does Raimond celebrate his father's life?

- How does the form of a memoir enable the exploration of interactions?

Christine

Christine is a German girl of sixteen when Romulus meets her and they fall in love. Physically Christine Anna Dorr was,

> Slightly shorter than average, she had black hair, a good figure, an open face with intense dark eyes and a musical voice...Men found her attractive beyond her physical features because of the way she combined vivacity and intense, haunted sadness. (p.6)

Christine, after she gives birth to Raimond, begins to exhibit signs of the mental and physical breakdown that would cloud her life. She cannot care for Raimond or any of her later children and 'feared she was doomed'. (p.9) A bad asthmatic she decides that

Australia is the place to go and the family emigrate. On the ship she shows signs of her promiscuous nature that is frowned upon by all who knew her, except her lovers.

Christine never settled at Frogmore and she began a long term affair with Mitru, which all caused all concerned much grief. She eventually moved to Melbourne with him but came to visit 'occasionally'. She was of little practical help around the house and 'was obviously and deeply depressed'. Neil Mikkelsen was the only local who spoke to Christine as the others disliked her for her neglect of Raimond. He recalled her,

> 'neat appearance and charming manner...very intelligent and a woman of substance. (p.31)

Christine's mental condition breaks down to the point she can barely function. Her decline leads her to undergo

> 'electric shock treatment that gave her no relief from the torment of her hallucinations.' (p.77)

Mitru wanted to marry her but she wasn't divorced from Romulus. Indeed, it seems at times, she hoped for reconciliation with Romulus. After Mitru suicides, she put the children in care and continued her unhappy life.

Raimond writes that,

> 'Tom Lillie and others disliked my mother partly because they saw her engaging vivacity as a dangerously seductive manifestation of a personality in a woman they believed to be entirely lacking in character.' (p.102)

Raimond thinks Christine was misunderstood and that women were 'vulnerable to the deadening attractions of middle class respectability.' (p.103) He thinks she may have been in the wrong 'conceptual environment' and that they didn't take her illness seriously enough.

Despite all this Romulus says,

'...he never loved a woman as much as my mother' (p.112).

Her influence led also to conflict between Romulus and Raimond, which took until 1981 to resolve. Indeed, her impact on their lives lasted until Raimond was reunited with his stepsisters many years later.

There can be no doubt that Christine impacted negatively on the lives around her. It is fortunate that the people with whom she interacted seemed to recover. She did not. It is interesting to note that the text concludes with the fact that his father was buried 'close to my mother'.

Questions for Christine

- Describe Christine's physical appearance in your own words.

- How do Mitru and Christine come to be together?

- Do you think that it is fair that Christine is disliked by the local folk because she is a hopeless parent?

- Support your response with evidence from the text.

- Do you agree with Raimond's interpretation that his mother was misunderstood?

Explain your response fully.

- Explain why you think that Romulus was buried close to Christine.

Hora

Hora as he is known in the text, was really Pantelimon Hora, a twenty four year old immigrant to Australia who meets Romulus in the camp. He was from Romania originally and was in Australia because he and his brother, Mitru, had fled the communists. They went to Yugoslavia first, then Italy and on to Australia.

Physically Hora,

> 'was particularly handsome. His high forehead, his large eyes and his mouth gave his face an aspect that reminded me years later of Albert Camus' (p.15)

It is mentioned that he was 'stronger in character' than his brother. Hora is known affectionately to Raimond as grosse Danciu and, at times through his life, acts as a father to him. For example when Romulus crashes the motorbike he comes to look after Raimond. This causes tension as Christine is in the house. He dislikes her and 'did not respect' her.(p.44)

Hora is kind to Raimond and Raimond comes to love him, especially after three months of care. Indeed, Hora saves Raimond from his father's anger and physical punishment. Hora's strength of character is also shown in how he deals with his brother's weakness over Christine, Romulus' breakdown and the loss of the two girls, Susan and Barbara, after Christine's death. It must be remembered that he also has a few mental health issues when a relationship of his own fails.

Hora and Romulus had similar philosophies about life and this is why they become firm friends. Part of this is the stories that he tells Raimond about great humanitarians such as Schweitzer and Semmelweis. We also see this philosophy in how he reacts to Solzhenitzyn's *The Gulag Archipelago*. Hora always had an,

'openness to the voices of others when they spoke with disciplined honesty from their own experiences' (p.73)

Hora took his views on life very seriously. He once stops talking to Raimond because if Raimond,

'was now such a shallow person, what could he say to me? How could he speak to me of anything that mattered?' (p.159)

Hora was strong in his beliefs and he always stuck with Romulus and his other friends. While he spoke the truth to his brother about Christine he was, of course, devastated by the suicide. They always seemed to overcome their quarrels and Hora despaired for his brother's life.

Hora later has a family of his own and he and Romulus drift apart partly because Hora,

'now suffered terribly from arthritis and found it difficult to drive' (p.195)

He sees Romulus on his final day and leaves after saying 'Goodbye' to his lifelong friend. Hora was a constant in Romulus' life and a mirror to him in many ways.

Questions for Hora

- Why do you think the relationship between Hora and Romulus is stronger than that between Mitru and Romulus?

- Why is Hora a father figure to Raimond?

- What does Raimond learn from their trips on the boat they built?

- How does Hora deal with his brother's relationship with Christine?

- How does Hora deal with Romulus' breakdown?

- Compose a paragraph that best describes Hora's philosophy on life.

Mitru

Mitru is the younger brother of Hora and was twenty-two when we first meet him in the book. Well educated, he fled from Romania to escape the communists and secure a passage to Australia. Mitru was of weaker character than his brother, Hora and physically different,

'the considerably shorter Mitru, with his slightly Asiatic eyes, slicked-down black hair and soft voice, reminded me of Peter Lorre'. (p.15)

Mitru forms a bond with Christine at Frogmore and Raimond writes that, at times, they appeared as a family. Eventually they moved to Melbourne and Raimond went with his mother. Raimond was fond of Mitru because,

'He was gentle, quick to laughter and with a wit that showed the sharpness and delicacy of his intelligence. I did not then, or ever, fully know the degree of his pain.' (p.26)

Mitru was haunted by Christine and he could not break away from her. He never understood her promiscuous nature and could not stop her taking lovers. This continues all through the relationship and drives him to finally commit suicide. Mitru felt guilty about his relationship with Christine and tried to reconcile his feelings in letters to Romulus.

Mitru wanted to marry Christine and this is especially so when she falls pregnant to him. Mitru wants Romulus to divorce her and he writes,

'In this situation neither she or I feel good and I think that you would not want this unpleasant situation to drag along as it is now.

More than that she is on her way to becoming a mother. To make it
easier for all of us...agree to give her a divorce.' (p.78)

Mitru does not get what he wants and Christine proves as hopeless a mother to their child as she was to Raimond. This becomes a point of contention, especially as she resumes her promiscuous nature after the baby is born. Mitru is so driven to distraction he attempts suicide by stabbing himself in the chest. He recovers and is made to promise he won't attempt it again.

This doesn't change anything and his demeanour gets worse. Hora tries to make him understand what is happening but to no avail, he won't leave her. He is driven to beating Christine with his belt and looking after the baby by himself. Raimond does not resent him for beating his mother because of his 'affection for him'.

One day he comes home early and argues with her over 'her neglect of Susan'. He beats her, takes Susan and then returns. Sadly he then,

'rode his bicycle to the Pioneer's Memorial Tower and dived fifteen
metres to his death. My mother was three months pregnant.' (p.91)

His death caused considerable grief and longing amongst his friends. He had to be buried by the Anglican priest as the Catholics wouldn't bury him because he took his own life. The funeral had an open coffin and this left a huge impression on Raimond,

'The memory of it haunted me for years' (p.92)

His death at twenty seven was tragic and his grave is marked with the epitaph,

'Belief in the afterlife is the only hope in us' (p.94)

Questions for Mitru

- Why do think the author makes it clear that Mitru has a weaker character than his brother, Hora?

- Describe Mitru and Christine's relationship in two paragraphs

- Why does Mitru ignore Hora's advice to leave Christine?

- There is much conjecture about Mitru's reasons for committing suicide.

- Why do you think he killed himself? Make specific references to the text.

- Do you think his epitaph sums up his life. Explain your response.

- Mitru experiences a number of interactions in his life. List these and categorise whether you think they were ultimately positive or negative.

Milka

Milka was a divorcee of Yugoslavian background who becomes Romulus' second wife and his companion until his death. They have an arranged meeting and Romulus is impressed with the twenty-nine year old woman. For him she was,

> *'just right, not too tall, not too short, not too fat, not too thin, not too dark, not too light.' (pp161-2)*

After their first meeting they continue to see each other and she comes to live with him at the Maryborough house in September 1963. They have a stormy relationship that sometimes results in physical battles.

Milka remained financially dependent throughout the marriage and Romulus respected this. They shared the work in the home and they marry six months after beginning to live together.

She has a great capacity for work and helps Romulus build the workshop. They also worked together inside with Milka helping him with the ironwork. They find separation difficult. Raimond believes that it was Milka who helped his father recover from his mental illness,

> *'To help him through his illness his strength of character needed the right kind of nurturing to function, and that, I believe, was given to him by the relative stability of his life with Milka.' (p.179)*

One of the great disappointments was that they could not have children and weren't allowed to adopt. Raimond thinks highly of Milka and 'warmed' to her immediately. He was very pleased she was there for his father. She and Romulus also share a love of the many animals that they kept around the house and on the property out of town.

Milka is portrayed in the text as a kind, hard-working woman who is loved and respected by Romulus.

Questions for Milka

- Where is Milka working when they meet?

- Why is their early relationship so difficult?

- List Milka's positive qualities as outlined by Raimond.

- How does Raimond perceive Milka?

Lydia

Lydia is a woman Romulus falls in love with through a series of letters that they exchange between Australia and Yugoslavia. She isn't physically present in much of the text but has a great impact on Romulus' life. This relationship begins in 1957 and Raimond records,

> 'She was in her early twenties, tall, slim, dark and very beautiful.
> (p.104)

The relationship blossoms and they make plans for the future including the fact that he would bring her and her mother and brother out to Australia. Romulus had fallen 'passionately' in love with her even though he had never met her. He was never 'more happy' and life was good for him.

This changed when he visits a woman who knows Lydia and has just come to Australia. She listens to his plans 'appalled' and tells him,

> 'to lay aside his plans. Lydia was not the woman he imagined her to be. On no account should he trust her. He must write to her and demand she tell him the truth.' (pp117-8)

Romulus writes to Lydia for the truth and finds she has already married and has been engaged to another man for a long time. Lydia has betrayed Romulus showing 'a malevolent human will'.

She later comes to Australia with her husband and Romulus decides to drive to Sydney to shoot the husband. He drives with Raimond to Sydney and when he knocks on the door Lydia opens it. Raimond is struck by her,

'She was even more beautiful than her photographs, gentle in every movement and in her speech, as delicate in manner as in her tall, slim, graceful figure. It was impossible to see the wickedness in her.' (p.139)

Romulus doesn't kill them. We never find out what motivated her to break her word, thus we are left to ponder her motivations. Whatever her motivation she has a profound impact on Romulus' life as her rejection sends him into a spiral of mental decay that ends with him being institutionalised.

Lydia is an enigmatic figure in the text. Even when her mother and brother come to live with Romulus nothing is explained except that Romulus still holds a deep passion for her. While she can be regarded a minor character, her interactions with Romulus lead to significant challenges and transformations for him.

Questions for Lydia

- How does Romulus and Lydia's relationship develop?

- Consider the following section of the 'Exploring Interactions' rubric, "students consider how acts of communication can shape, challenge or transform attitudes and beliefs, identities and behaviours." How did Romulus' communication with Lydia and the woman who knew Lydia, shape, challenge and/ or transform Romulus?

- What does Lydia promise and how does Romulus find out she lied?

- What motive do you think Lydia might have had for lying to Romulus?

Vacek

Vacek Vilkouikas was a Lithuanian who sold Romulus the Sunbeam motorbike. They met at Cairn Curran and when the camp was broken up he lived,

> *'in the hills outside Maldon, between two granite boulders sealed with corrugated iron, branches and bits of timber...Not far from this rude shelter he built a small shed in which he kept awful concoctions that he had cooked, sometimes in his own urine.'*
> *(pp65-6)*

Vacek became more and more insane as time passed but was considered harmless. He used to drop into Frogmore and stay but would come and go as fancy took him. He was a 'gentle' person who had 'a dreamy, poetic nature' (p.66).

He also felt a close bond with animals and used to talk to them and think that he could read signs in their behaviour. He wanted the best for people and Raimond never seems worried about him through the course of the text.

With his condition worsening he leaves Romulus' employ and seems to wander the country, finally settling back in Maldon. Unfortunately for him times, had changed and now he was institutionalised as a certified psychiatric patient.

Vacek begins to like life in the institutions and when he is able to leave he doesn't. He stays

> *'there and in reception homes in the community for the rest of his life.'* (p.143)

Vacek is a colourful character in the text and he plays a small but insightful role in the lives of Romulus and Raimond. His 'odd' behaviours are tolerated well by them and he is living proof of their tolerant and accepting philosophy.

Questions on Vacek

- Where does Vacek meet Romulus?

- Where does Vacek live in Maldon? Use your own words to describe his abode.

- Summarise Vacek's philosophy of life.

- How does Vacek come to be institutionalised?

THEMATIC CONCERNS

- Exploring Interactions
- Migrant Experience and Cultural Values
- Family
- Personal Ethos

Exploring Interactions

Go back and refresh yourself with the rubric and module outline included at the beginning of this guide. The questions you will be asked will stem from the rubric. Exploring Interactions, the elective title, is basically about the manner in which people live, interact and connect with each other in a variety of situations. The rubric asks for a little more in that it states,

'These contexts may include the home, cultural, friendship and sporting groups, the workplace and the digital world. Through exploring their prescribed text and texts of their own choosing, students consider how acts of communication can shape, challenge or transform attitudes and beliefs, identities and behaviours. In their responding and composing, students develop their understanding of how the social context of individuals' interactions can affect perceptions of ourselves and others, relationships and society.'

P.14 BOSTES Prescriptions document at

HTTP://WWW.BOARDOFSTUDIES.NSW.EDU.AU/SYLLABUS_HSC/PDF_DOC/ENGLISH-
PRESCRIPTIONS-2015-20.PDF

What this means for our study of Gaita's *Romulus, My Father* is that we need to focus on how the characters interact in a variety of contexts, including familial, social and cultural. Explore what changes these interactions result in for characters in terms of how they view the world and others.

An initial reaction when exploring interactions must be the psychological effects of change and stress. Mental illness is a theme that permeates the novel and impacts on all the characters in one way or another. We have read examples in the character studies and seen the impact of suicide, depression and paranoia on the lives of the sufferer and those who care for them. These illnesses affect their personal lives detrimentally e.g. Christine's infidelities, Hora's suicide and jealousy and Romulus' hospitalization. Such issues also affect the manner in which they relate to people and the manner in which people react to them. Christine is never understood in the countryside, Romulus is regarded as an outsider and we read of the continuous misunderstandings and issues caused by the negative impact of their psychology.

Another effect of this damaged psyche is the ability to manage on an economic level. Not only are characters hampered by being in a new country but these problems inhibit, and at times, disable their ability to work. Often, we read these characters are unable to cope in the workplace due to the constraints of depression. Thus, they struggle to even provide themselves with proper care, no matter how hard they try. This further alienates them from society and even makes them fall foul of the law.

Also, mis-communication is a real issue in the novel and it is sometimes due to language, sometimes culture and often due to differences in beliefs and attitudes. Romulus has extremely profound personal beliefs which he lives and expresses and which often lead him into conflict. He loves strongly, perhaps too well, which also causes misunderstandings. What was valuable in his past is not so in the future and his ability to adapt is taken away by circumstances.

Even the strong friendships that Romulus forges bring him heartache and strength in a paradoxical manner. He needs them yet he suffers because of them. His wife re-partners with his friend and he seems to search for meaning perpetually. Culturally Romulus is drawn to a small circle of people and results from language and cultural heritage. He seems estranged from Australian life as he struggles to establish himself and to secure Raimond a place in the world.

These conflicts are clearly delineated in the relationship between Romulus and Raimond. Raimond is a 'product' if you like of Australia, more so than many of the other characters we meet. He has an excellent grasp of Australian mores and culture which enables him to see the problems. He can't communicate these to his father effectively and they come into conflict. We see alienation between the two and then reconciliation as circumstances and time enable both to change. Perspectives are transformed and attitudes mellow as they grow to see the world differently.

We must also consider how these interactions in society change the way characters perceive the world. For them, the migrant experience can result in interactions with places seen as alien and hostile place and where they are misunderstood. We will examine this in detail in the next section with specific examples.

Migrant Experience and Cultural Values

Romulus and Christine migrated to Australia and found the values, beliefs and attitudes entirely different from their previous life in Europe. This changed how they interacted with each other and with those around them. The first example of this is in how Romulus was treated at work and the expectations of him,

> *'Perhaps for good reason, or perhaps merely as an expression of their prejudice against 'New Australians' (as immigrants were called) ...the camp chose not to utilise the many skills of the foreign workers who were invariably given menial manual tasks.'*
> *(p.116)*

These 'Balts' as they were called were resigned to this treatment and 'had long come to accept what fate dealt'. Cultural differences are also evident in simple things such as the distance and isolation of the country while different life experiences are also highlighted,

> *'Without thinking, responding to the instinct of an immigrant unused to the tinder-dry conditions of an Australian summer, he set fire to the stook in order to kill the snake...The local newspaper ridiculed the New Australian for his folly' (p.28)*

As well as these simple cultural differences that the family experienced it was the conservatism of the country that affected them, especially Christine, who was desperately lonely and had little human contact out in the bush,

'He was one of the few people in the area who liked her, most having taken against her for her neglect of me.' (p.31)

She was not liked and indeed people were 'hostile' to her. She also caused problems in the community by wandering off and this exacerbated the problem. Christine never 'fitted in' to Australian society and even to Hora she had become a 'characterless' woman. Raimond writes,

> *'But for someone like my mother, highly intelligent, deeply sensuous,, anarchic and unstable, this emphasis on character, given an Australian accent, provided the wrong conceptual environment for her to find herself and others to understand her'*
> *(p.103)*

It is mentioned elsewhere in the text that in the context of Australia at that time it was not a conducive period for migrants to show their best,

> *'Those were the days before multi-culturalism – immigrants were tolerated, but seldom accorded the respect they deserved. It occurred to few of the men and women of Central Victoria that the foreigners in their midst might live their lives and judge their surroundings in the light of standards which were equal and sometimes superior to theirs.' (p.100)*

These cultural differences show the contrast in different ways of thinking. The focus on cultural and conceptually differences and resultant deep misunderstandings are evidence of ineffective interactions. Different ways of living were judged rather than accepted according to Gaita and this causes discomfort for the migrants.

It is important, however, to note that not everything is negative. Romulus and Hora were 'appreciative of the tolerance show to them by Australians'. Hora also couldn't believe the freedom and tolerance' he discovered in Australia. Not all were negative towards them. The economic freedoms that were available in Australia allowed them to thrive. Even in his old age when Romulus returns to Yugoslavia he,

> 'complained about the rudeness, verging on brutality...He thought services were appalling and spent a miserable night waiting to be attended in a hospital in which patients lay on sheets smeared with other people's faeces.' (pp170-1)

He returns to Australia with a 'renewed appreciation of life in Australia'. Toward the end of the text Gaita notes that 'attitudes to New Australians had changed' and that,

> 'My father noted this, but he and Milka were nonetheless glad of the change, recognising its generosity, and the same distinctive Australian decency that he had known in many of the people he met when he lived at Frogmore.' (p.183)

This text castes some light on the immigrant experience and cultural differences that occurred in a specific period of Australian history. It shows one migrant family's experience of Australia and how both cultures interacted.

Questions for Migrant Experience and Cultural Values

- Describe one incident that shows different ways of thinking between the two cultures.

- Research life in Australia during the 1950s.

- What types of cultural activities were happening? Do you think it would have been a difficult time for a person to immigrate to Australia and adapt?

- Why do you think Christine had such difficulties interacting in Australia?

- Do you think Gaita's is an accurate portrayal of Australian life at the time?

Family Interactions

Family is a theme that runs consistently through *Romulus, My Father* and the text shows families at their best and worst. The strongest impression that the text conveys is that family is the most important thing and this extends to relatives and an extended family. Even though the Gaita's family is dislocated and has difficulties, it is family that individuals come back to and it is here that the interactions are strongest.

Even Christine wants, near the end of her life, to be united with Romulus and has hopes of reconciliation. Raimond admits he had little sense of family until he visited his mother's sister, Maria, after a twenty- year separation. All Maria can say is 'What a surprise' and this visit changes Raimond's feelings,

> *'This newfound sense of family, my love for Maria and her children, Ulrich and Andrea, gradually awakened in me a desire to find Susan and Barbara.' (p.193)*

This results in a need to seek out his 'lost' step-sisters, the daughters of Mitru and Christine who had been given out for adoption. Both had seemingly been lost to the family after their parents suicided. Hora was especially sad that he had lost contact with his brother's children and it is these interactions that are important to him. It is an intriguing sideline that Barbara and Susan 'were astonished and confused' they had a brother but were 'reunited, nervously but happily.' Familial interactions had significant consequences and strengthened bonds.

The people who were the happiest at this reunion were Hora and Romulus who both knew the value of family and its worth. Romulus, for example, believed, *'for brother and sister not to know of each other's whereabouts, let alone existence, was so profoundly against the order of things that it constituted a metaphysical damage to their lives. When Barbara and Susan came with me to Maryborough...he felt the damage had been repaired.' (p.193)*

We see this sense of family in Romulus' life when he helps others and enjoys company round at his home. His life also seems completed by his more consistent relationship with Milka and it is sad that their desire for a family is thwarted.

Sense of family is also seen in the community when Christine is disliked for not fulfilling her requirements as a mother. Her illness doesn't enable her to act as a good mother and this has many repercussions in her life. In many ways she is punished for her lack of family sensibilities at times. Christine faces the common beliefs of the time and she breaks many of the social taboos. Her interactions are coloured by this in a negative way.

Family strength, resiliance and bonds are shown in this non-fiction text but so too is the fragility of familial interactions.

Questions for Family Interactions

- How do you see Raimond's family?

- Imagine you are Susan or Barbara. How do you feel after being told that you have a brother? Try to describe your emotions but also how you intend to deal with your new family.

- What does Milka do for Raimond's well-being?

- Choose one of the following and describe Raimond's relationship with them.
  - Romulus
  - Christine
  - Milka
  - Barbara/Susan

Personal Ethos

The philosophical bent of the text shows not only the training of the author but reflects the views of the central figure of this biography, Romulus. Romulus had a strong personal ethos which he lived by and it was like a code of honour which had to be followed. This was also shown in the character of Hora who had a similar ethos.

Hora for example teaches Raimond stories about,

> *'men with ideals, devoted to science or humanity, and who were persecuted by an arrogant and complacent establishment that cried 'Humbug". (p.71)*

Much of Hora and Romulus' time together was spent discussing issues. In these discussions they showed their 'individuality' and Raimond learns much, especially,

> *'the connection between individuality and character and the connection between these of 'having something to say' of seeing another person as being fully and distinctively another perspective on the world. (p.73)*

These discussions reveal values and beliefs and the code the men lived by. Their core values enabled them to deal with a variety of situations and interactions, although not always positively.

For Romulus it was also his work that defined his character and was an expression of it. Romulus sees his work as an extension of himself. Raimond says of him,

'Like him his work was honest through and through' (p.98)

He goes on to state how Romulus always took full responsibility for his work and how his reputation grew because of it. Many of his positive interactions can be associated with his work and his business ethics.

This personal ethos was central to Romulus' life and to some extent explains how he cannot understand Lydia's duplicity. Note how he keeps his word on bringing Lydia's mother and brother to Australia and how he supports people from his homeland despite their hypocrisy.

Romulus felt that there were 'few things more important than a good name' (p.99) and he worked for this. This whole ethos was at the core of his being and it helped him get through his breakdown.

Gaita makes much of this personal integrity in the text and shows how it affects more than the individual yet it should/can be at every individual's core. Much of the text is devoted to this and more detailed analyses for specific characters are given in the character section.

Questions for Personal Ethos

- Do you think the quote below is an accurate description of Romulus? Explain your response fully.

  'Like him his work was honest through and through' (p.98)

- Describe Hora's personal ethos and how it impacted on his ability to interact with others. You might also discuss how it impacted on the way he viewed people and certain situations.

- How was Romulus' work a good indication of his character? How does his work provide a way of interacting positively with others?

LANGUAGE ANALYSIS

Gaita's level of education is evident in the text through the concepts he discusses and also the sophisticated vocabulary used to analyse those concepts. It is also relevant to note that Gaita develops a sense of education in the main characters in the text so that the conversations rarely border on the colloquial. Even his mother is portrayed as educated and Romulus self- educated.

It is also important that all the major characters in the text are from migrant/middle European backgrounds so the slang and Australian vernacular we would expect from this period of time is missing. Certainly the common terminology from blue- collar workers, which these people are, is absent.

There are also few long conversations related in the text and these are merely retold as narrative or short snippets are included. This may be for two reasons. The first is that the passage of time has erased the details in Gaita's mind or secondly, that the narrative moves more quickly without dialogue. We must also remember that these events are from Gaita's perspective only. This means there is a natural bias in the recount of events – Raimond is only a child for much of it and not privy to some events.

Another factor to consider when discussing language is that although it is an adult voice in the text the memories are childhood ones. Thus the sophisticated language is used to colour the early memories that would have been perceived differently at the time. Many of the anecdotes in the text are now seen with the perspective of time and occasionally this shows in the intellectual/analytical analysis of very emotive events. For example the analytical way he examines his mother's suicide expunges all the childhood sadness he must have felt,

'She killed herself only days after their conversation' (p.111)

Raimond Gaita goes on to write how she died; 'asphyxiation' and about his 'numb' emotions at her burial.

Interestingly Gaita also does emote quite clearly at times and is less reflective. He describes his affection for Mitru, Hora, Milka and, of course, his father. He reveals emotion when he sees his father in hospital, both after his accidents and in Ballarat after his breakdown. He also describes his emotions as his father dies,

'I sat down to wait with him for his death. The nurses brought me a comfortable chair, one that would open into a bed, in case I slept the night. I reflected that just as I had been with him alone at Frogmore during the time of his terrible affliction, so now I was alone with him in his mortal agony.' (p.205)

Gaita's biography of Romulus' life doesn't gloss over the 'weaknesses' in his family background. Many biographies, especially those of siblings and relatives, try to gloss over difficulties and issues. The point of Gaita's text is to use these problems to analyse and philosophise and then to expound a personal viewpoint.

We not only get Gaita's view of life but he clearly enunciates his father's, Hora's and Vacek's. These are all very similar and are based on a non-judgmental, accepting philosophy that understands the differences in individuals. Indeed Gaita criticises Australian society for not having this view, *'other sharp divisions, it could not capture the many worthy ways of being human. It nourished some possibilities, maimed others and would not allow some to see the light of day. Women particularly suffered under it.' (p.103)*

He describes it as 'puritanism' but it needs to be remembered this is just an opinion based on personal experience not facts. Indeed many people regard the period he writes as a golden period in Australian history. His views are based on the migrant experience and personal experience. His view is rather different from the majority of people who lived in the period. Gaita's family and extended group are quite dysfunctional and this may have also coloured the experience.

The language of *Romulus, My Father* is very expressive and gives the reader a clear indication of the characters through its physical and character descriptions. Good examples of these are given in the character analysis section of this study guide. What this text does however is give, more than other biographies, gives a philosophical and cultural to events and decisions. This shows us the characters in a rounded, multi-dimensional way. It also emphasises Gaita's intelligence in his ability to perceive both people and times.

Questions for Language

- Create a list of words that show Gaita's excellent vocabulary.

- Why do you think Gaita includes only snippets of conversation rather than full conversations?

- Do you think his descriptions of places such as Frogmore are well written? Why/why not? Explain your answer with close reference to the text.

- Choose one passage and analyse how it shows emotion by close analysis of the language used.

- How has Gaita's chosen profession as a philosopher intruded into the text?

ESSAY QUESTION

Read carefully the question below and then examine the essay outline on the following pages. Try to develop your essay along these lines and develop strategies to answer any questions you might encounter.

A list of these response types is given at the end of the sample essay. Look at these and you should be familiar with most of them. Try to practice them when you can and develop your writing skills.

QUESTION

'Discuss how Romulus, My Father and one text of your own choosing explore the interactions between characters.

Discuss this statement with close reference to the text and the cultural and social contexts which affect these interactions.

THE ESSAY

The essay has been the subject of numerous texts and you should have the basic form well in hand. As teachers, the point we would emphasise would be to link the paragraphs both to each other and back to your argument (which should directly respond to the question). Of course ensure your argument is logical and sustained.

Make sure you use specific examples and that your quotes are accurate. To ensure that you respond to the question make sure you plan carefully and are sure what relevant point each paragraph is making. It is solid technique to actually 'tie up' each point by explicitly coming back to the question.

When composing an essay the basic conventions of the form are:

> - State your argument, outline the points to be addressed and perhaps have a brief definition.

> A solid structure for each paragraph is:
> - Topic sentence (the main idea and its link to the previous paragraph/ argument)
> - Explanation / discussion of the point including links between texts if applicable.
> - Detailed evidence (Close textual reference- quotes, incidents and technique discussion.)
> - Tie up by restating the point's relevance to argument / question

> - Summary of points
> - Final sentence that restates your argument

As well as this basic structure you will need to focus on:

Audience – for the essay the audience must be considered formal unless specifically stated otherwise. Therefore your language must reflect the audience. This gives you the opportunity to use the jargon and vocabulary that you have learnt in English. For the audience ensure your introduction is clear and has impact. Avoid slang or colloquial language including contractions (like doesn't, e.g., etc.).

Purpose – the purpose of the essay is to answer the question given. The examiner evaluates how well you can make an argument and understand the module's issues and its text(s). An essay is solidly structured so its composer can analyse ideas. This is where you earn marks. It does not retell the story or state the obvious.

Communication – Take a few minutes to plan the essay. If you rush into your answer it is almost certain you will not make the most of the brief 40 minutes to show all you know about the question. More likely you will include irrelevant details that do not gain you marks but waste your precious time. Remember an essay is formal so do not do the following: story-tell, list and number points, misquote, use slang or colloquial language, be vague, use non sentences or fail to address the question.

ESSAY OUTLINE – *ROMULUS, MY FATHER*

'Discuss how Romulus, My Father and one text of your own choosing explore the interactions between characters.

Discuss this statement with close reference to the text and the cultural and social contexts which affect these interactions.

A few notes about the question:

- Remember the actual question is asking you what you have learned about the interactions in the play.

- The statement that follows the initial statement is to point you in the right direction.

- It is important you take note of the ideas the statement raises and check your response does address them.

- Take care you use the number of texts the examiner asks for. There is no value in writing on more and you will definitely be penalised for writing on less.

- You MUST have quotations and textual references that show you have a good knowledge and understanding of your prescribed AND related text.

- Your response must look at BOTH WHAT the texts have taught you about the importance of exploring interactions AND HOW the composer represented those ideas.

PLAN: Don't even think about starting without one!

Introduce...

the texts you are using in the response

Definition:

Explanation of exploring interactions and their impact in the texts

- Argument: *Romulus, My Father* and one ORT is able to communicate these interactions:
- Between people
- They are changed by context etc.

You need to let the marker know what texts you are discussing. It is good to start with your definition but it could have come in the first paragraph of the body. You MUST state your argument in response to the question and the points you will cover as part of it. Don't wait until the end of the response to give it!

↓

Idea 1- People interact and change how they see others and the world

- explain the idea
- where and how shown in *Romulus, My Father* and one ORT
- relevance to modern audiences

Idea 2- People interact in different ways depending on context etc.

- explain the idea
- where and how shown in *Romulus, My Father* and one ORT
- Explain techniques i.e. how.
- relevance to modern audience

You can use the things you have learned to organise the essay. For each one you say where you saw this in your prescribed text and where in the other text.

Two ideas are usually enough as you can explore them in detail.

↓

- Summary of two key ideas
- Final sentence that restates your argument

Make sure your conclusion restates your argument. It does not have to be too long.

© Five Senses Education Pty Ltd

EXPLORING INTERACTIONS: OTHER RELATED TEXTS

Prose Fiction

Town by James Roy (2007)

Thirteen interwoven short stories from thirteen adolescents set over thirteen months in an unnamed Australian country town. This text explores the interactions of these young adults in a school and a wider community setting. The text deals with contemporary hard hitting issues such as disability, family, death and grief, racism and sexuality. Readers slowly begin to see how the world each character inhabits is shaped by their peers around them and through interactions both great and small.

A Long Way Down by Nick Hornby (2005)

Four strangers meet on New Year's Eve on top of a London building where they plan to jump and end their lives. However, the four instead, form a sort of surrogate family that helps them stay alive and work through their issues. This text uses multiple viewpoints to delve deeper into each character's psyche and propel the plot forward. It is through the interactions of four very different people we begin to explore how these people transform their view on the world and set themselves free from dark places.

Deadly, Unna? by Phillip Gwynne (1998)

This novel explores cross cultural interactions and uses the game of Australian Rules Football to explore racism in a small South Australian coastal town. The novel also explores the interaction between sporting life and community life and how they play into one another. As the novel progresses we see understanding of the other raise in our protagonist, while racial tensions come to a head with other characters. The novel manages to blend sport with a relevant social message that stresses the importance of communication in order for positive change to happen.

Gone Girl by Gillian Flynn (2012)

A compelling crime thriller that moves its plot along through the viewpoint of two main characters. As we watch the two interact through a series of first-hand experiences and diary entries we begin to unravel this complicated mystery. Character interactions are multi-faceted and we start to realise everyone is not who they seem. This is a text that explores the complicated relationships between human beings and how different forms of communication can be used to manipulate.

The Slap by Christos Tsiolkas (2008)

At a family BBQ a man slaps a child who is not his own, what follows are eight viewpoints that show the effects of that one incident and how it has changed lives/interactions/relationships forever. This text explores the new multi-cultural Australia and how one incident can shape us and the way we see the world. The author is interested in how a very different group of people from different cultures, religions, sexualities and belief systems learn to live and interact with one another when they all have a different opinion on what is right and what is wrong.

Film

Crash directed by Paul Haggis (2004)

A film about social and racial tensions that takes course over two days in Los Angeles, as we see character's stories interweave and interact with one another. The interactions between these characters force the audience to question racial stereotypes while at the same type acknowledge the truth that some of these stereotypes contain.

As the title suggests, the film shows its characters colliding and crashing, sometimes metaphorically and sometimes literally. It is through these interactions a bleak, yet realistic portrait of humanity is painted.

American Beauty directed by Sam Mendes (1999)

An American drama that looks deeper into the seemingly normal suburban life of several characters. Marital and generational conflict is explored as we look closely at the lives of these people and their interactions with one another.

The film exposes the flaws of the 'American Dream' and how the lack of meaningful interaction and connection can lead to isolation. The film also fantastically juxtaposes a variety of both positive and negative connections between characters and explores their impacts on these people.

Lars and the Real Girl directed by Craig Gillespie (2007)

A delusional young man, Lars, strikes up a romantic relationship with a doll he finds on the internet. Lars struggles to interact and relate to the community around him but manages to find a meaningful existence with this plastic doll. Through the interaction between Lars and the doll and the way the community interact with Lars and accepts this strange situation, the importance of community, compassion and the importance of understanding one another is revealed.

Her directed by Spike Jonze (2013)

Set in the not so distant future, an introverted man, Theodore, sparks up a relationship with an advanced artificially intelligent operating system. What starts as a friendship soon turns to love. While many texts explore how technology is making it harder for us to interact with one another, this film shows how technology can connect us on a level deeper than ever before. Through the interaction between Theodore and the operating system "Samantha" we learn that technological interactions can not only strengthen relationships but fulfil emotional needs.

Songs

Father and Son written and performed by Cat Stevens (1970)

A song that explores generational difference and conflict through interaction in form of a conversation between a father and son who hold very different views about life and what can be gained from life. The listener is presented with two distinct voices and listen to both men express their indifference towards one another. Stevens uses tone of voice perfectly to paint two different characters and showcase the generational differences that occur and how we can challenge what others believe.

URL Badman written and performed by Lily Allen (2014)

A contemporary pop song that explores interactions between young people, specifically young men who sit at home on the internet attacking others. Allen uses satire, sarcasm, wit and contemporary references to poke fun at the cyber culture that belittles others safely behind a computer screen and keyboard. She exposes the meaningless interactions that occur online and hits back at cyber bullying.

Drama

Wolf Lullaby written by Hilary Bell (1996)

An Australian play that questions human nature ane sources of evil. How do we as human beings interact with one another when we are on the edge and in high pressure situations? When the blame of a brutal murder falls upon nine year old Lizzie in a remote Australian town, characters' lives are forever changed as they come to terms and question whether or not Lizzie is capable of such a crime. Through their interactions with Lizzie, the adults begin to question their accepted beliefs and what humans are really capable of.

Poetry

"I Cannot Forget"

Two poems by Alexander Kimel, holocaust survivor. http://remember.org/witness/kimel2

Picture Books

The Island by Armin Greder

The Rabbits by Shaun Tan

Short Film

Look Up by Gary Turk (2014)

A short film that utilises spoken word and visual techniques to warn us of the dangers of the digital culture. The narrator stresses that we no longer interact with one another in reality but more with our digital devices, and by doing this we are missing out on the world around us and an abundance of experiences.

Using irony, Turk expresses how inventions that were designed to connect us, have actually isolated us more and he believes we need to get back to more meaningful interactions that are based in reality.

Just A Friend by Sophia Thakur and Chozen (2013)

A short film that uses poetry and spoken word to explore the interaction between a young couple that are experiencing an issue that affects many couples, trust. Using poetic language the couple express their feelings toward each other and if they can trust each other. We watch them interact and follow their body language, facial expressions and other visual techniques, using these as further clues to piece their interaction together and whether or not they can get through their problems.

With thanks to Michael Ursino